JOHN KEATS

'Ode to a Nightingale'
and other poems

JOHN KEATS

'Ode to a Nightingale' and other poems

Selected and introduced by

DOMINIQUE ENRIGHT

Michael O'Mara Books Limited

First published in Great Britain in 2002 by
Michael O'Mara Books Limited
9 Lion Yard, Tremadoc Road
London SW4 7NQ

A CIP catalogue record for this book is available from the British Library

The text of Keats's poems as printed here follows accepted available editions

ISBN 1-85479-655-0

1 3 5 7 9 10 8 6 4 2

Designed and typeset by Martin Bristow
Printed and bound in Finland by WS Bookwell, Juva

CONTENTS

INTRODUCTION

JOHN KEATS died from consumption in Rome in February 1821. He was twenty-five years old. His life was as tragic as it was short: one after the other, his parents and then his grandparents (with whom he and his brothers and sister lived) died, as, later, did his younger brother, Tom, whom he nursed through the last months of tuberculosis; passionately and unhappily in love with Fanny Brawne, he became engaged to her not long before his own death. Arguably the greatest of all the English Romantic poets, he left behind him an astonishingly large body of work almost as remarkable for its maturity as for its beauty. 'How soon the film of death obscured that eye, Whence Genius mildly flashed,' lines from his sonnet 'To Chatterton', might so aptly be applied to Keats himself.

Keats believed that poetry should reach out to the heart – the senses – and not to the mind, to conscious thought. Whether in his longer narrative works like 'The Eve of St Agnes', or in such sonnets as 'On First Looking Into Chapman's *Homer*', or in his magnificent odes such as those 'To a Nightingale' and 'To Autumn', his verse resonates with lyricism and with sensuous imagery, however melancholy his tone or his subject. His finest poems are among the greatest in the language; almost all of them strike a chord in the heart of even the most jaded reader.

This compact selection includes many of his greatest shorter poems, as well as extracts from longer works. Such a brief collection can never do proper justice to the full enchantment of Keats's verse; it is hoped, however, that it will allow readers a satisfying taste of the riches of his work.

Dedication. To Leigh Hunt, Esq.
(1817)

Glory and loveliness have pass'd away;
   For if we wander out in early morn,
   No wreathèd incense do we see upborne
Into the east, to meet the smiling day:
No crowd of nymphs soft voic'd and young, and gay,
   In woven baskets bringing ears of corn,
   Roses, and pinks, and violets, to adorn
The shrine of Flora in her early May.
But there are left delights as high as these.
   And I shall ever bless my destiny,
That in a time when under pleasant trees
   Pan is no longer sought, I feel a free
A leafy luxury, seeing I could please,
   With these poor offerings, a man like thee.

How many bards gild the lapses of time!
(1817)

How many bards gild the lapses of time!
A few of them have ever been the food
Of my delighted fancy, – I could brood
Over their beauties, earthly, or sublime:
And often, when I sit me down to rhyme,
These will in throngs before my mind intrude;
   But no confusion, no disturbance rude
Do they occasion; 'tis a pleasing chime.
So the unnumber'd sounds that evening store;
   The songs of birds – the whisp'ring of the leaves –
   The voice of waters – the great bell that heaves
With solemn sound, – and thousand others more,
   That distance of recognizance bereaves,
Make pleasing music, and not wild uproar.

On First Looking into Chapman's *Homer*
(1817)

Much have I travell'd in the realms of gold,
   And many goodly states and kingdoms seen;
   Round many western islands have I been
Which bards in fealty to Apollo hold.
Oft of one wide expanse had I been told
   That deep-brow'd Homer ruled as his demesne:
   Yet did I never breathe its pure serene
Till I heard Chapman speak out loud and bold:
Then felt I like some watcher of the skies
   When a new planet swims into his ken;
Or like stout Cortez when with eagle eyes
   He stared at the Pacific – and all his men
Look'd at each other with a wild surmise –
   Silent, upon a peak in Darien.

To Chatterton
(1817)

O Chatterton! how very sad thy fate!
   Dear child of sorrow – son of misery!
   How soon the film of death obscured that eye,
Whence Genius mildly flashed, and high debate.
How soon that voice, majestic and elate,
   Melted in dying numbers! Oh! how nigh
   Was night to thy fair morning. Thou didst die
A half-blown flow'ret which cold blasts amate.
But this is past: thou art among the stars
   Of highest heaven: to the rolling spheres
   Thou sweetest singest: nought thy hymning mars,
Above the ingrate world and human fears.
   On earth the good man base detraction bars
From thy fair name, and waters it with tears.

A Thing of Beauty is a Joy For Ever,
from Book 1 of *Endymion*
(1818)

A thing of beauty is a joy for ever:
Its loveliness increases; it will never
Pass into nothingness; but still will keep
A bower quiet for us, and a sleep
Full of sweet dreams, and health, and quiet breathing.
Therefore, on every morrow, are we wreathing
A flowery band to bind us to the earth,
Spite of despondence, of the inhuman dearth
Of noble natures, of the gloomy days,
Of all the unhealthy and o'er-darken'd ways
Made for our searching: yes, in spite of all,
Some shape of beauty moves away the pall
From our dark spirits. Such the sun, the moon,
Trees old and young, sprouting a shady boon
For simple sheep; and such are daffodils
With the green world they live in; and clear rills
That for themselves a cooling covert make
'Gainst the hot season; the mid-forest brake,
Rich with a sprinkling of fair musk-rose blooms:
And such too is the grandeur of the dooms
We have imagined for the mighty dead;

All lovely tales that we have heard or read:
An endless fountain of immortal drink,
Pouring unto us from the heaven's brink.

Nor do we merely feel these essences
For one short hour; no, even as the trees
That whisper round a temple become soon
Dear as the temple's self, so does the moon,
The passion poesy, glories infinite,
Haunt us till they become a cheering light
Unto our souls, and bound to us so fast
That, whether there be shine or gloom o'ercast,
They always must be with us, or we die.

Therefore, 'tis with full happiness that I
Will trace the story of Endymion.
The very music of the name has gone
Into my being, and each pleasant scene
Is growing fresh before me as the green
Of our own valleys: so I will begin
Now while I cannot hear the city's din;
Now while the early budders are just new,
And run in mazes of the youngest hue
About old forests; while the willow trails
Its delicate amber; and the dairy pails

Bring home increase of milk. And, as the year
Grows lush in juicy stalks, I'll smoothly steer
My little boat, for many quiet hours,
With streams that deepen freshly into bowers.

Many and many a verse I hope to write,
Before the daisies, vermeil rimm'd and white,
Hide in deep herbage; and ere yet the bees
Hum about globes of clover and sweet peas,
I must be near the middle of my story.
O may no wintry season, bare and hoary,
See it half-finish'd: but let Autumn bold,
With universal tinge of sober gold,
Be all about me when I make an end.
And now at once, adventuresome, I send
My herald thought into a wilderness:
There let its trumpet blow, and quickly dress
My uncertain path with green, that I may speed
Easily onward, thorough flowers and weed.

O Solitude! If I Must With Thee Dwell
(1817)

O Solitude! if I must with thee dwell,
  Let it not be among the jumbled heap
  Of murky buildings: climb with me the steep, –
Nature's observatory – whence the dell,
In flowery slopes, its river's crystal swell,
  May seem a span; let me thy vigils keep
  'Mongst boughs pavilion'd, where the deer's swift leap
Startles the wild bee from the foxglove bell.
But though I'll gladly trace these scenes with thee,
  Yet the sweet converse of an innocent mind,
  Whose words are images of thoughts refined,
Is my soul's pleasure; and it sure must be
  Almost the highest bliss of human-kind,
When to thy haunts two kindred spirits flee.

Ode to Psyche
(1820)

O Goddess! hear these tuneless numbers, wrung
   By sweet enforcement and remembrance dear,
And pardon that thy secrets should be sung
   Even into thine own soft-conchèd ear:
Surely I dreamt to-day, or did I see
   The wingèd Psyche with awaken'd eyes?
I wander'd in a forest thoughtlessly,
   And, on the sudden, fainting with surprise,
Saw two fair creatures, couchèd side by side
   In deepest grass, beneath the whisp'ring roof
   Of leaves and trembled blossoms, where there ran
     A brooklet, scarce espied:

'Mid hush'd, cool-rooted flowers, fragrant-eyed,
   Blue, silver-white, and budded Tyrian,
They lay calm-breathing on the bedded grass;
   Their arms embracèd, and their pinions too;
   Their lips touch'd not, but had not bade adieu,
As if disjoinèd by soft-handed slumber,
And ready still past kisses to outnumber
   At tender eye-dawn of aurorean love:

The wingèd boy I knew;
But who wast thou, O happy, happy dove?
   His Psyche true!

O latest-born and loveliest vision far
  Of all Olympus' faded hierarchy!
Fairer than Phoebe's sapphire-region'd star,
  Or Vesper, amorous glow-worm of the sky;
Fairer than these, though temple thou hast none,
    Nor altar heap'd with flowers;
Nor virgin-choir to make delicious moan
    Upon the midnight hours;
No voice, no lute, no pipe, no incense sweet
  From chain-swung censer teeming;
No shrine, no grove, no oracle, no heat
  Of pale-mouth'd prophet dreaming.

O brightest! though too late for antique vows,
  Too, too late for the fond believing lyre,
When holy were the haunted forest boughs,
  Holy the air, the water, and the fire;
Yet even in these days so far retired
  From happy pieties, thy lucent fans,
  Fluttering among the faint Olympians,
I see, and sing, by my own eyes inspired.

So let me be thy choir, and make a moan
    Upon the midnight hours;
Thy voice, thy lute, thy pipe, thy incense sweet
   From swingèd censer teeming;
Thy shrine, thy grove, thy oracle, thy heat
   Of pale-mouth'd prophet dreaming.

Yes, I will be thy priest, and build a fane
   In some untrodden region of my mind,
Where branchèd thoughts, new grown with pleasant pain,
   Instead of pines shall murmur in the wind:
Far, far around shall those dark-cluster'd trees
   Fledge the wild-ridgèd mountains steep by steep;
And there by zephyrs, streams, and birds, and bees,
   The moss-lain Dryads shall be lull'd to sleep;
And in the midst of this wide quietness
   A rosy sanctuary will I dress
With the wreath'd trellis of a working brain,
   With buds, and bells, and stars without a name,
With all the gardener Fancy e'er could feign,
   Who breeding flowers, will never breed the same:
And there shall be for thee all soft delight
   That shadowy thought can win,
A bright torch, and a casement ope at night,
   To let the warm Love in!

La Belle Dame Sans Merci
(1820)

O what can ail thee, knight-at-arms,
   Alone and palely loitering?
The sedge has withered from the lake,
   And no birds sing.

O what can ail thee, knight-at-arms!
   So haggard and so woebegone?
The squirrel's granary is full,
   And the harvest's done.

I see a lily on thy brow
   With anguish moist and fever dew,
And on thy cheek a fading rose
   Fast withereth too.

'I met a lady in the meads,
Full beautiful – a faery's child,
Her hair was long, her foot was light,
And her eyes were wild.

I made a garland for her head,
    And bracelets too, and fragrant zone;
She look'd at me as she did love,
And made sweet moan.

I set her on my pacing steed,
    And nothing else saw all day long,
For sidelong would she bend, and sing
    A faery's song.

She found me roots of relish sweet,
    And honey wild, and manna dew,
And sure in language strange she said
"I love thee true."

She took me to her elfin grot,
    And there she wept, and sighed full sore,
And there I shut her wild wild eyes
    With kisses four.

And there she lullèd me asleep,
And there I dream'd – Ah! woe betide!
The latest dream I ever dream'd
On the cold hill's side.

I saw pale kings and princes too,
    Pale warriors, death-pale were they all;
They cried – "La Belle Dame sans Merci
Hath thee in thrall!"

I saw their starv'd lips in the gloam,
    With horrid warning gapèd wide,
And I awoke and found me here,
    On the cold hill's side.

And this is why I sojourn here,
    Alone and palely loitering,
Though the sedge has wither'd from the lake,
    And no birds sing.'

From The Eve of St Agnes

(1820)

I

St Agnes' Eve – Ah, bitter chill it was!
The owl, for all his feathers, was a-cold;
The hare limp'd trembling through the frozen grass,
And silent was the flock in woolly fold:
Numb were the Beadsman's fingers, while he told
His rosary, and while his frosted breath,
Like pious incense from a censer old,
Seem'd taking flight for heaven, without a death,
Past the sweet Virgin's picture, while his prayer he saith.

IV

That ancient Beadsman heard the prelude soft;
And so it chanc'd, for many a door was wide,
From hurry to and fro. Soon, up aloft,
The silver, snarling trumpets 'gan to chide:
The level chambers, ready with their pride,
Were glowing to receive a thousand guests:
The carvèd angels, ever eager-eyed,
Star'd, where upon their heads the cornice rests,
With hair blown back, and wings put cross-wise on their breasts.

V

At length burst in the argent revelry,
With plume, tiara, and all rich array,
Numerous as shadows haunting fairily
The brain, new stuff'd, in youth, with triumphs gay
Of old romance. These let us wish away,
And turn, sole-thoughted, to one Lady there,
Whose heart had brooded, all that wintry day,
On love, and wing'd St Agnes' saintly care,
As she had heard old dames full many times declare.

VI

They told her how, upon St Agnes' Eve,
Young virgins might have visions of delight,
And soft adorings from their loves receive
Upon the honey'd middle of the night,
If ceremonies due they did aright;
As, supperless to bed they must retire,
And couch supine their beauties, lily white;
Nor look behind, nor sideways, but require
Of Heaven with upward eyes for all that they desire.

VII

Full of this whim was thoughtful Madeline:
The music, yearning like a God in pain,
She scarcely heard: her maiden eyes divine,
Fix'd on the floor, saw many a sweeping train
Pass by – she heeded not at all: in vain
Came many a tiptoe, amorous cavalier,
And back retir'd; not cool'd by high disdain,
But she saw not: her heart was otherwhere:
She sigh'd for Agnes' dreams, the sweetest of the year.

VIII

She danc'd along with vague, regardless eyes,
Anxious her lips, her breathing quick and short:
The hallow'd hour was near at hand: she sighs
Amid the timbrels, and the throng'd resort
Of whisperers in anger, or in sport;
'Mid looks of love, defiance, hate, and scorn,
Hoodwink'd with faery fancy; all amort,
Save to St Agnes and her lambs unshorn,
And all the bliss to be before to-morrow morn.

IX

So, purposing each moment to retire,
She linger'd still. Meantime, across the moors,
Had come young Porphyro, with heart on fire
For Madeline. Beside the portal doors,
Buttress'd from moonlight, stands he, and implores
All saints to give him sight of Madeline,
But for one moment in the tedious hours,
That he might gaze and worship all unseen;
Perchance speak, kneel, touch, kiss – in sooth such things
       have been.

X

He ventures in: let no buzz'd whisper tell:
All eyes be muffled, or a hundred swords
Will storm his heart, Love's fev'rous citadel:
For him, those chambers held barbarian hordes,
Hyena foemen, and hot-blooded lords,
Whose very dogs would execrations howl
Against his lineage: not one breast affords
Him any mercy, in that mansion foul,
Save one old beldame, weak in body and in soul.

XI

Ah, happy chance! the aged creature came,
Shuffling along with ivory-headed wand,
To where he stood, hid from the torch's flame,
Behind a broad hall pillar, far beyond
The sound of merriment and chorus bland:
He startled her; but soon she knew his face,
And grasp'd his fingers in her palsied hand,
Saying, 'Mercy, Porphyro! hie thee from this place;
They are all here to-night, the whole blood-thirsty race!'

XIV

'St Agnes! Ah! it is St Agnes' Eve –
Yet men will murder upon holy days:
Thou must hold water in a witch's sieve,
And be liege-lord of all the Elves and Fays,
To venture so: it fills me with amaze
To see thee, Porphyro! – St Agnes' Eve!
God's help! my lady fair the conjuror plays
This very night: good angels her deceive!
But let me laugh awhile, I've mickle time to grieve.'

XV

Feebly she laugheth in the languid moon,
While Porphyro upon her face doth look,
Like puzzled urchin on an aged crone
Who keepeth clos'd a wond'rous riddle-book,
As spectacled she sits in chimney nook.
But soon his eyes grew brilliant, when she told
His lady's purpose; and he scarce could brook
Tears, at the thought of those enchantments cold,
And Madeline asleep in lap of legends old.

XXIV

A casement high and triple-arch'd there was,
All garlanded with carven imag'ries
Of fruits, and flowers, and bunches of knot-grass,
And diamonded with panes of quaint device,
Innumerable of stains and splendid dyes,
As are the tiger-moth's deep-damask'd wings;
And in the midst, 'mong thousand heraldries,
And twilight saints, and dim emblazonings,
A shielded scutcheon blush'd with blood of queens and kings.

XXV

Full on this casement shone the wintry moon,
And threw warm gules on Madeline's fair breast,
As down she knelt for heaven's grace and boon;
Rose-bloom fell on her hands, together prest,
And on her silver cross soft amethyst,
And on her hair a glory, like a saint:
She seem'd a splendid angel, newly drest,
Save wings, for heaven: – Porphyro grew faint:
She knelt, so pure a thing, so free from mortal taint.

XXVII

Soon, trembling in her soft and chilly nest,
In sort of wakeful swoon, perplex'd she lay,
Until the poppied warmth of sleep oppress'd
Her soothed limbs, and soul fatigued away;
Flown, like a thought, until the morrow-day;
Blissfully haven'd both from joy and pain;
Clasp'd like a missal where swart Paynims pray;
Blinded alike from sunshine and from rain,
As though a rose should shut, and be a bud again.

XXX

And still she slept an azure-lidded sleep,
 In blanchèd linen, smooth, and lavender'd,
 While he from forth the closet brought a heap
 Of candied apple, quince, and plum, and gourd;
 With jellies soother than the creamy curd,
 And lucent syrops, tinct with cinnamon;
 Manna and dates, in argosy transferr'd
 From Fez; and spicèd dainties, every one,
From silken Samarcand to cedar'd Lebanon.

XXXI

These delicates he heap'd with glowing hand
 On golden dishes and in baskets bright
 Of wreathèd silver: sumptuous they stand
 In the retired quiet of the night,
 Filling the chilly room with perfume light. —
 'And now, my love, my seraph fair, awake!
 Thou art my heaven, and I thine eremite:
 Open thine eyes, for meek St Agnes' sake,
Or I shall drowse beside thee, so my soul doth ache.'

XXXIII

Awakening up, he took her hollow lute, –
Tumultuous, – and, in chords that tenderest be,
He play'd an ancient ditty, long since mute,
In Provence call'd, 'La belle dame sans mercy':
Close to her ear touching the melody; –
Wherewith disturb'd, she utter'd a soft moan:
He ceased – she panted quick – and suddenly
Her blue affrayèd eyes wide open shone:
Upon his knees he sank, pale as smooth-sculptured stone.

XXXIV

Her eyes were open, but she still beheld,
Now wide awake, the vision of her sleep:
There was a painful change, that nigh expell'd
The blisses of her dream so pure and deep
At which fair Madeline began to weep,
And moan forth witless words with many a sigh;
While still her gaze on Porphyro would keep;
Who knelt, with joinèd hands and piteous eye,
Fearing to move or speak, she look'd so dreamingly.

XXXV

'Ah, Porphyro!' said she, 'but even now
Thy voice was at sweet tremble in mine ear,
Made tuneable with every sweetest vow;
And those sad eyes were spiritual and clear:
How chang'd thou art! how pallid, chill, and drear!
Give me that voice again, my Porphyro,
Those looks immortal, those complainings dear!
Oh leave me not in this eternal woe,
For if thou diest, my Love, I know not where to go.'

XXXVII

'Tis dark: quick pattereth the flaw-blown sleet:
'This is no dream, my bride, my Madeline!'
'Tis dark: the icèd gusts still rave and beat:
'No dream, alas! alas! and woe is mine!
Porphyro will leave me here to fade and pine. –
Cruel! what traitor could thee hither bring?
I curse not, for my heart is lost in thine,
Though thou forsakest a deceivèd thing; –
A dove forlorn and lost with sick unprunèd wing.'

XXXVIII

'My Madeline! sweet dreamer! lovely bride!
Say, may I be for aye thy vassal blest?
Thy beauty's shield, heart-shaped and vermeil dyed?
Ah, silver shrine, here will I take my rest
After so many hours of toil and quest,
A famish'd pilgrim, – saved by miracle.
Though I have found, I will not rob thy nest
Saving of thy sweet self; if thou think'st well
To trust, fair Madeline, to no rude infidel.

XXXIX

'Hark! 'tis an elfin-storm from faery land,
Of haggard seeming, but a boon indeed:
Arise – arise! the morning is at hand; –
The bloated wassaillers will never heed: –
Let us away, my love, with happy speed;
There are no ears to hear, or eyes to see, –
Drown'd all in Rhenish and the sleepy mead.
Awake! arise! my love, and fearless be,
For o'er the southern moors I have a home for thee.'

XL

She hurried at his words, beset with fears,
For there were sleeping dragons all around,
At glaring watch, perhaps, with ready spears.
Down the wide stairs a darkling way they found;
In all the house was heard no human sound.
A chain-droop'd lamp was flickering by each door;
The arras, rich with horseman, hawk, and hound,
Flutter'd in the besieging wind's uproar;
And the long carpets rose along the gusty floor.

XLI

They glide, like phantoms, into the wide hall;
Like phantoms, to the iron porch they glide;
Where lay the Porter, in uneasy sprawl,
With a huge empty flagon by his side;
The wakeful bloodhound rose, and shook his hide,
But his sagacious eye an inmate owns:
By one, and one, the bolts full easy slide: –
The chains lie silent on the footworn stones; –
The key turns, and the door upon its hinges groan.

And they are gone: ay, ages long ago
These lovers fled away into the storm.
That night the Baron dreamt of many a woe,
And all his warrior-guests, with shade and form
Of witch, and demon, and large coffin-worm,
Were long be-nightmar'd. Angela the old
Died palsy-twitch'd, with meagre face deform;
The Beadsman, after thousand aves told,
For aye unsought-for slept among his ashes cold.

Written in the Cottage where Burns was born

This mortal body of a thousand days
Now fills, O Burns, a space in thine own room,
Where thou didst dream alone on budded bays,
Happy and thoughtless of thy day of doom!
My pulse is warm with thine own Barley-bree,
My head is light with pledging a great soul,
My eyes are wandering, and I cannot see
Fancy is dead and drunken at its goal;
Yet can I stamp my foot upon thy floor,
Yet can I ope thy window-sash to find
The meadow thou hast trampèd o'er and o'er, –
Yet can I think of thee till thought is blind, –
Yet can I gulp a bumper to thy name, –
O smile among the shades, for this is fame!

Ode on a Grecian Urn
(1820)

Thou still unravish'd bride of quietness!
  Thou foster-child of Silence and slow Time,
Sylvan historian, who canst thus express
  A flow'ry tale more sweetly than our rhyme:
What leaf-fring'd legend haunts about thy shape
  Of deities or mortals, or of both,
    In Tempe or the dales of Arcady?
  What men or gods are these? What maidens loth?
What mad pursuit? What struggle to escape?
  What pipes and timbrels? What wild ecstasy?

Heard melodies are sweet, but those unheard
  Are sweeter: therefore, ye soft pipes, play on;
Not to the sensual ear, but, more endear'd,
  Pipe to the spirit ditties of no tone:
Fair youth, beneath the trees, thou canst not leave
  Thy song, nor ever can those trees be bare;
    Bold Lover, never, never canst thou kiss,
Though winning near the goal – yet, do not grieve;
    She cannot fade, though thou hast not thy bliss,
  For ever wilt thou love, and she be fair!

Ah, happy, happy boughs! that cannot shed
　　Your leaves, nor ever bid the spring adieu;
And, happy melodist, unwearièd,
　　For ever piping songs for ever new;
More happy love! more happy, happy love!
　　For ever warm and still to be enjoy'd,
　　　For ever panting and for ever young;
All breathing human passion far above,
　　That leaves a heart high-sorrowful and cloyed,
　　　A burning forehead, and a parching tongue.

Who are these coming to the sacrifice?
　　To what green altar, O mysterious priest,
Lead'st thou that heifer lowing at the skies,
　　And all her silken flanks with garlands drest?
What little town by river or sea-shore,
　　Or mountain-built with peaceful citadel,
　　　Is emptied of its folk, this pious morn?
And, little town, thy streets for evermore
　　Will silent be; and not a soul to tell
　　　Why thou art desolate, can e'er return.

O Attic shape! Fair attitude! with brede
   Of marble men and maidens overwrought,
With forest branches and the trodden weed;
   Thou, silent form, dost tease us out of thought
As doth eternity: Cold Pastoral!
   When old age shall this generation waste,
      Thou shalt remain, in midst of other woe
   Than ours, a friend to man, to whom thou sayst,
'Beauty is truth, truth beauty, – that is all
      Ye know on earth, and all ye need to know.'

The day is gone
(1819)

The day is gone, and all its sweets are gone!
    Sweet voice, sweet lips, soft hand, and softer breast,
Warm breath, light whisper, tender semi-tone,
    Bright eyes, accomplish'd shape, and lang'rous waist!
Faded the flower and all its budded charms,
    Faded the sight of beauty from my eyes,
Faded the shape of beauty from my arms,
    Faded the voice, warmth, whiteness, paradise –
Vanish'd unseasonably at shut of eve,
    When the dusk holiday – or holinight
Of fragrant-curtain'd love begins to weave
    The woof of darkness thick, for hid delight;
But, as I've read love's missal through to-day,
    He'll let me sleep, seeing I fast and pray.

Ode to a Nightingale

(1820)

My heart aches, and a drowsy numbness pains
  My sense, as though of hemlock I had drunk,
Or emptied some dull opiate to the drains
  One minute past, and Lethe-wards had sunk:
'Tis not through envy of thy happy lot,
  But being too happy in thy happiness, —
    That thou, light-wingèd Dryad of the trees,
      In some melodious plot
  Of beechen green, and shadows numberless,
    Singest of summer in full-throated ease.

O for a draught of vintage! that hath been
  Cooled a long age in the deep-delved earth,
Tasting of Flora and the country green,
  Dance, and Provençal song, and sunburnt mirth!
O for a beaker full of the warm South,
  Full of the true, the blushful Hippocrene,
    With beaded bubbles winking at the brim
      And purple-stainèd mouth;
  That I might drink, and leave the world unseen,
    And with thee fade away into the forest dim:

Fade far away, dissolve, and quite forget
    What thou among the leaves hast never known,
The weariness, the fever, and the fret
        Here, where men sit and hear each other groan;
Where palsy shakes a few, sad, last grey hairs,
    Where youth grows pale, and spectre-thin, and dies;
        Where but to think is to be full of sorrow
                And leaden-eyed despairs;
    Where Beauty cannot keep her lustrous eyes,
        Or new Love pine at them beyond to-morrow.

Away! away! for I will fly to thee,
    Not charioted by Bacchus and his pards,
But on the viewless wings of Poesy,
    Though the dull brain perplexes and retards:
Already with thee! tender is the night,
    And haply the Queen-Moon is on her throne,
        Cluster'd around by all her starry Fays;
                But here there is no light,
Save what from heaven is with the breezes blown
    Through verdurous glooms and winding mossy ways.

I cannot see what flowers are at my feet,
    Nor what soft incense hangs upon the boughs,
But, in embalmèd darkness, guess each sweet
    Wherewith the seasonable month endows
The grass, the thicket, and the fruit-tree wild;
    White hawthorn, and the pastoral eglantine;
        Fast-fading violets covered up in leaves;
            And mid-May's eldest child,
    The coming musk-rose, full of dewy wine,
        The murmurous haunt of flies on summer eves.

Darkling I listen; and for many a time
    I have been half in love with easeful Death,
Call'd him soft names in many a musèd rhyme,
    To take into the air my quiet breath;
Now more than ever seems it rich to die,
    To cease upon the midnight with no pain,
        While thou art pouring forth thy soul abroad
            In such an ecstasy!
    Still wouldst thou sing, and I have ears in vain –
        To thy high requiem become a sod.

Thou wast not born for death, immortal Bird!
  No hungry generations tread thee down;
The voice I hear this passing night was heard
  In ancient days by emperor and clown:
Perhaps the self-same song that found a path
    Through the sad heart of Ruth, when, sick for home,
      She stood in tears amid the alien corn;
          The same that oft-times hath
      Charm'd magic casements, opening on the foam
    Of perilous seas, in faery lands forlorn.

Forlorn! the very word is like a bell
  To toll me back from thee to my sole self!
Adieu! the fancy cannot cheat so well
  As she is famed to do, deceiving elf.
Adieu! adieu! thy plaintive anthem fades
    Past the near meadows, over the still stream,
      Up the hill-side; and now 'tis buried deep
          In the next valley-glades:
      Was it a vision, or a waking dream?
        Fled is that music: – do I wake or sleep?

If by Dull Rhymes Our English Must be Chain'd
(On the Sonnet)
(1819)

If by dull rhymes our English must be chain'd,
    And, like Andromeda, the Sonnet sweet
Fetter'd, in spite of pained loveliness;
Let us find out, if we must be constrain'd,
    Sandals more interwoven and complete
To fit the naked foot of poesy;
Let us inspect the lyre, and weigh the stress
Of every chord, and see what may be gain'd
    By ear industrious, and attention meet;
Misers of sound and syllable, no less
Than Midas of his coinage, let us be
    Jealous of dead leaves in the bay wreath crown;
So, if we may not let the Muse be free,
    She will be bound with garlands of her own.

Ode on Melancholy
(1820)

No, no! go not to Lethe, neither twist
    Wolf's-bane, tight-rooted, for its poisonous wine;
Nor suffer thy pale forehead to be kiss'd
    By nightshade, ruby grape of Proserpine;
Make not your rosary of yew-berries,
    Nor let the beetle, nor the death-moth be
        Your mournful Psyche, nor the downy owl
A partner in your sorrow's mysteries;
    For shade to shade will come too drowsily,
        And drown the wakeful anguish of the soul.

But when the melancholy fit shall fall
    Sudden from heaven like a weeping cloud,
That fosters the droop-headed flowers all,
    And hides the green hill in an April shroud;
Then glut thy sorrow on a morning rose,
    Or on the rainbow of the salt sand-wave,
        Or on the wealth of globèd peonies;
Or if thy mistress some rich anger shows,
    Emprison her soft hand, and let her rave,
        And feed deep, deep upon her peerless eyes.

She dwells with Beauty — Beauty that must die;
   And Joy, whose hand is ever at his lips
Bidding adieu; and aching Pleasure nigh,
   Turning to poison while the bee-mouth sips:
Ay, in the very temple of Delight
   Veil'd Melancholy has her sovran shrine,
     Though seen of none save him whose
       strenuous tongue
   Can burst Joy's grape against his palate fine:
His soul shall taste the sadness of her might,
   And be among her cloudy trophies hung.

Sonnet to a Cat

(1818)

Cat! who hast pass'd thy grand climacteric,
   How many mice and rats hast in thy days
   Destroy'd? – How many tit bits stolen? Gaze
With those bright languid segments green, and prick
Those velvet ears – but pr'ythee do not stick
   Thy latent talons in me – and upraise
   Thy gentle mew – and tell me all thy frays
Of fish and mice, and rats and tender chick.
Nay, look not down, nor lick thy dainty wrists –
   For all the wheezy asthma, – and for all
Thy tail's tip is nick'd off – and though the fists
   Of many a maid have given thee many a maul,
Still is that fur as soft as when the lists
   In youth thou enter'dst on glass-bottled wall.

Sonnet: Why did I laugh to-night?
(1819)

Why did I laugh to-night? No voice will tell:
 No God, no Demon of severe response,
Deigns to reply from heaven or from Hell.
 Then to my human heart I turn at once.
Heart! Thou and I are here, sad and alone;
 I say, why did I laugh! O mortal pain!
O Darkness! Darkness! ever must I moan,
 To question Heaven and Hell and Heart in vain.
Why did I laugh? I know this Being's lease,
 My fancy to its utmost blisses spreads;
Yet would I on this very midnight cease,
 And the world's gaudy ensigns see in shreds;
Verse, Fame, and Beauty are intense indeed,
 But Death intenser – Death is Life's high meed.

Two Sonnets on Fame

(1819)

I

Fame, like a wayward girl, will still be coy
    To those who woo her with too slavish knees,
But makes surrender to some thoughtless boy,
    And dotes the more upon a heart at ease;
She is a Gipsy will not speak to those
    Who have not learnt to be content without her;
A Jilt, whose ear was never whisper'd close,
    Who thinks they scandal her who talk about her;
A very Gipsy is she, Nilus-born,
    Sister-in-law to jealous Potiphar;
Ye love-sick Bards! repay her scorn for scorn;
    Ye Artists lovelorn! madmen that ye are!
Make your best bow to her and bid adieu,
Then, if she likes it, she will follow you.

II

'You cannot eat your cake and have it too.' – Proverb

How fever'd is the man, who cannot look
    Upon his mortal days with temperate blood,
Who vexes all the leaves of his life's book,
    And robs his fair name of its maidenhood;
It is as if the rose should pluck herself,
    Or the ripe plum finger its misty bloom,
As if a Naiad, like a meddling elf,
    Should darken her pure grot with muddy gloom;
But the rose leaves herself upon the briar,
    For winds to kiss and grateful bees to feed,
And the ripe plum still wears its dim attire;
    The undisturbèd lake has crystal space;
    Why then should man, teasing the world for grace,
Spoil his salvation for a fierce miscreed?

To Fanny

(1819)

I cry your mercy – pity – love! – aye, love!
  Merciful love that tantalizes not,
One-thoughted, never-wandering, guileless love,
  Unmask'd, and being seen – without a blot!
O! let me have thee whole, – all – all – be mine!
  That shape, that fairness, that sweet minor zest
Of love, your kiss, – those hands, those eyes divine,
  That warm, white, lucent, million-pleasured breast, –
Yourself – your soul – in pity give me all,
  Withhold no atom's atom or I die,
Or living on, perhaps, your wretched thrall,
  Forget, in the mist of idle misery,
Life's purposes, – the palate of my mind
Losing its gust, and my ambition blind!

Fancy

(1820)

Ever let the Fancy roam,
Pleasure never is at home:
At a touch sweet Pleasure melteth,
Like to bubbles when rain pelteth;
Then let wingèd Fancy wander
Through the thought still spread beyond her:
Open wide the mind's cage door,
She'll dart forth, and cloudward soar,
O sweet Fancy! let her loose;
Summer's joys are spoilt by use,
And the enjoying of the Spring
Fades as does its blossoming;
Autumn's red-lipp'd fruitage too,
Blushing through the mist and dew,
Cloys with tasting: What do then?
Sit thee by the ingle, when
The sear faggot blazes bright,
Spirit of a winter's night;
When the soundless earth is muffled,
And the cakèd snow is shuffled
From the ploughboy's heavy shoon;
When the Night doth meet the Noon

In a dark conspiracy
To banish Even from her sky.
Sit thee there, and send abroad,
With a mind self-overaw'd,
Fancy, high-commission'd: – send her!
She has vassals to attend her:
She will bring, in spite of frost,
Beauties that the earth hath lost;
She will bring thee, all together,
All delights of summer weather;
All the buds and bells of May,
From dewy sward or thorny spray;
All the heapèd Autumn's wealth,
With a still, mysterious stealth:
She will mix these pleasures up
Like three fit wines in a cup,
And thou shalt quaff it:– thou shalt hear
Distant harvest-carols clear;
Rustle of the reapèd corn;
Sweet birds antheming the morn:
And, in the same moment – hark!
'Tis the early April lark,
Or the rooks, with busy caw,
Foraging for sticks and straw.
Thou shalt, at one glance, behold

The daisy and the marigold;
White-plumed lilies, and the first
Hedge-grown primrose that hath burst;
Shaded hyacinth, alway
Sapphire queen of the mid-May;
And every leaf, and every flower
Pearlèd with the self-same shower.
Thou shalt see the field-mouse peep
Meagre from its cellèd sleep;
And the snake all winter-thin
Cast on sunny bank its skin;
Freckled nest-eggs thou shalt see
Hatching in the hawthorn-tree,
When the hen-bird's wing doth rest
Quiet on her mossy nest;
Then the hurry and alarm
When the bee-hive casts its swarm;
Acorns ripe down-pattering,
While the autumn breezes sing.

Oh, sweet Fancy! let her loose;
Every thing is spoilt by use:
Where's the cheek that doth not fade,
Too much gazed at? Where's the maid
Whose lip mature is ever new?

Where's the eye, however blue,
Doth not weary? Where's the face
One would meet in every place?
Where's the voice, however soft,
One would hear so very oft?
At a touch sweet Pleasure melteth
Like to bubbles when rain pelteth.
Let, then, wingèd Fancy find
Thee a mistress to thy mind:
Dulcet-eyed as Ceres' daughter,
Ere the God of Torment taught her
How to frown and how to chide;
With a waist and with a side
White as Hebe's, when her zone
Slipt its golden clasp, and down
Fell her kirtle to her feet,
While she held the goblet sweet,
And Jove grew languid. – Break the mesh
Of the Fancy's silken leash;
Quickly break her prison-string
And such joys as these she'll bring.–
Let the wingèd Fancy roam,
Pleasure never is at home.

I had a dove

I had a dove and the sweet dove died;
And I have thought it died of grieving:
O, what could it grieve for? its feet were tied,
With a silken thread of my own hand's weaving.

Sweet little red feet, why should you die?
Why should you leave me, sweet bird, why?
You liv'd alone in the forest-tree,
Why, pretty thing! would you not live with me?
I kiss'd you oft and gave you white peas;
Why not live sweetly, as in the green trees?

You Say You Love

I

You say you love; but with a voice
   Chaster than a nun's, who singeth
The soft Vespers to herself
   While the chime-bell ringeth –
     O love me truly!

II

You say you love; but with a smile
   Cold as sunrise in September,
As you were Saint Cupid's nun,
   And kept his weeks of Ember.
     O love me truly!

III

You say you love – but then your lips
   Coral tinted teach no blisses.
More than coral in the sea –
   They never pout for kisses –
     O love me truly!

IV

You say you love; but then your hand
   No soft squeeze for squeeze returneth,
It is like a statue's, dead, –
   While mine for passion burneth –
    O love me truly!

V

O breathe a word or two of fire!
   Smile, as if those words should burn me,
Squeeze as lovers should – O kiss
   And in thy heart inurn me!
    O love me truly!

His Last Sonnet (Sonnet written on a Blank Page in Shakespeare's Poems)
(1819)

Bright star, would I were stedfast as thou art! –
   Not in lone splendour hung aloft the night,
And watching, with eternal lids apart,
   Like Nature's patient, sleepless Eremite,
The moving waters at their priestlike task
   Of pure ablution round earth's human shores,
Or gazing on the new soft fallen mask
   Of snow upon the mountains and the moors –
No – yet still stedfast, still unchangeable,
   Pillow'd upon my fair love's ripening breast,
To feel for ever its soft fall and swell,
   Awake for ever in a sweet unrest,
Still, still to hear her tender-taken breath,
And so live ever – or else swoon to death.

When I have fears
(1818)

When I have fears that I may cease to be
  Before my pen has glean'd my teeming brain,
Before high-pilèd books, in charact'ry,
  Hold like rich garners the full-ripen'd grain;
When I behold, upon the night's starr'd face,
  Huge cloudy symbols of a high romance,
And feel that I may never live to trace
  Their shadows, with the magic hand of chance;
And when I feel, fair creature of an hour!
  That I shall never look upon thee more,
Never have relish in the faery power
  Of unreflecting love! – then on the shore
Of the wide world I stand alone, and think
Till Love and Fame to nothingness do sink.

Ode to Fanny

Physician Nature! let my spirit blood!
O ease my heart of verse and let me rest;
Throw me upon thy Tripod, till the flood
Of stifling numbers ebbs from my full breast.
A theme! a theme! great nature! give a theme;
   Let me begin my dream.
I come – I see thee, as thou standest there,
Beckon me not into the wintry air.

Ah! dearest love, sweet home of all my fears,
And hopes, and joys, and panting miseries, –
To-night, if I may guess, thy beauty wears
   A smile of such delight,
   As brilliant and as bright,
As when with ravish'd, aching, vassal eyes,
   Lost in soft amaze,
     I gaze, I gaze!

Who now, with greedy looks, eats up my feast?
What stare outfaces now my silver moon!
Ah! keep that hand unravish'd at the least;

Let, let, the amorous burn –
　　But pr'ythee, do not turn
The current of your heart from me so soon.
　　O! save, in charity,
　　The quickest pulse for me.

Save it for me, sweet love! though music breathe
Voluptuous visions into the warm air;
Though swimming through the dance's dangerous wreath:
　　Be like an April day,
　　Smiling and cold and gay,
A temperate lily, temperate as fair;
　　Then, Heaven! there will be
　　A warmer June for me.

Why, this, you'll say, my Fanny! is not true:
Put your soft hand upon your snowy side,
Where the heart beats: confess – 'tis nothing new –
　　Must not a woman be
　　A feather on the sea,
Sway'd to and fro by every wind and tide?
　　Of as uncertain speed
　　As blow-ball from the mead?

I know it – and to know it is despair
To one who loves you as I love, sweet Fanny!
Whose heart goes flutt'ring for you every where,
   Nor, when away you roam,
   Dare keep its wretched home,
   Love, love alone, his pains severe and many:
Then, loveliest! keep me free,
From torturing jealousy.

Ah! if you prize my subdued soul above
The poor, the fading, brief, pride of an hour;
Let none profane my Holy See of love,
   Or with a rude hand break
   The sacramental cake:
Let none else touch the just new-budded flower;
   If not – may my eyes close,
   Love! on their lost repose.

Ode to Autumn
(1820)

Season of mists and mellow fruitfulness!
   Close bosom-friend of the maturing sun;
Conspiring with him how to load and bless
   With fruit the vines that round the thatch-eaves run;
To bend with apples the moss'd cottage-trees,
   And fill all fruit with ripeness to the core;
     To swell the gourd, and plump the hazel shells
   With a sweet kernel; to set budding more,
And still more, later flowers for the bees,
Until they think warm days will never cease,
   For Summer has o'erbrimmed their clammy cells.

Who hath not seen thee oft amid thy store?
   Sometimes whoever seeks abroad may find
Thee sitting careless on a granary floor,
   Thy hair soft-lifted by the winnowing wind;
Or on a half-reap'd furrow sound asleep,
   Drows'd with the fume of poppies, while thy hook
     Spares the next swath and all its twinèd flowers;

And sometimes like a gleaner thou dost keep
    Steady thy laden head across a brook;
    Or by a cider-press, with patient look,
    Thou watchest the last oozings, hours by hours.

Where are the songs of Spring? Ay, where are they?
    Think not of them, thou hast thy music too,
        While barrèd clouds bloom the soft-dying day
And touch the stubble-plains with rosy hue;
    Then in a wailful choir the small gnats mourn
    Among the river sallows, borne aloft
        Or sinking as the light wind lives or dies;
And full-grown lambs loud bleat from hilly bourn;
    Hedge-crickets sing, and now with treble soft
    The redbreast whistles from a garden-croft;
        And gathering swallows twitter in the skies.

Stanzas: In drear-nighted December

In drear-nighted December,
Too happy, happy tree,
Thy branches ne'er remember
Their green felicity:
The north cannot undo them
With a sleety whistle through them,
Nor frozen thawings glue them
From budding at the prime.

In drear-nighted December,
Too happy, happy brook,
Thy bubblings ne'er remember
Apollo's summer look;
But with a sweet forgetting
They stay their crystal fretting,
Never, never petting
About the frozen time.

Ah, would 'twere so with many
A gentle girl and boy!
But were there ever any
Writhed not at passèd joy?
The feel of not to feel it,
When there is none to heal it,
Nor numbed sense to steel it,
Was never said in rhyme.

To Hope
(1815)

When by my solitary hearth I sit,
When no fair dreams before my mind's eye flit,
And the bare heath of life presents no bloom;
Sweet Hope, ethereal balm upon me shed,
And wave thy silver pinions o'er my head.

Whene'er I wander, at the fall of night,
Where woven boughs shut out the moon's bright ray,
Should sad Despondency my musings fright,
And frown, to drive fair Cheerfulness away,
Peep with the moon-beams through the leafy roof,
And keep that fiend Despondence far aloof.

Should Disappointment, parent of Despair,
Strive for her son to seize my careless heart;
When, like a cloud, he sits upon the air,
Preparing on his spell-bound prey to dart:
Chase him away, sweet Hope, with visage bright,
And fright him as the morning frightens night!

Whene'er the fate of those I hold most dear
Tells to my fearful breast a tale of sorrow,
O bright-eyed Hope, my morbid fancy cheer;
Let me awhile thy sweetest comforts borrow:
Thy heaven-born radiance around me shed,
And wave thy silver pinions o'er my head!

Should e'er unhappy love my bosom pain,
From cruel parents, or relentless fair;
O let me think it is not quite in vain
To sigh out sonnets to the midnight air!
Sweet Hope, ethereal balm upon me shed,
And wave thy silver pinions o'er my head!

In the long vista of the years to roll,
Let me not see our country's honour fade:
O let me see our land retain her soul,
Her pride, her freedom; and not freedom's shade.
From thy bright eyes unusual brightness shed –
Beneath thy pinions canopy my head!

Let me not see the patriot's high bequest,
Great Liberty! how great in plain attire!
With the base purple of a court oppress'd,
Bowing her head, and ready to expire:
But let me see thee stoop from heaven on wings
That fill the skies with silver glitterings!

And as, in sparkling majesty, a star
Gilds the bright summit of some gloomy cloud;
Brightening the half veil'd face of heaven afar:
So, when dark thoughts my boding spirit shroud,
Sweet Hope, celestial influence round me shed,
Waving thy silver pinions o'er my head.

To Some Ladies
(1817)

What though while the wonders of nature exploring,
I cannot your light, mazy footsteps attend;
Nor listen to accents, that almost adoring,
Bless Cynthia's face, the enthusiast's friend:

Yet over the steep, whence the mountain stream rushes,
With you, kindest friends, in idea I rove;
Mark the clear tumbling crystal, its passionate gushes,
Its spray that the wild flower kindly bedews.

Why linger you so, the wild labyrinth strolling?
Why breathless, unable your bliss to declare?
Ah! you list to the nightingale's tender condoling,
Responsive to sylphs, in the moon beamy air.

'Tis morn, and the flowers with dew are yet drooping,
I see you are treading the verge of the sea:
And now! ah, I see it – you just now are stooping
To pick up the keep-sake intended for me.

If a cherub, on pinions of silver descending,
Had brought me a gem from the fret-work of heaven;
And smiles, with his star-cheering voice sweetly blending,
The blessings of Tighe had melodiously given;

It had not created a warmer emotion
Than the present, fair nymphs, I was blest with from you
Than the shell, from the bright golden sands of the ocean
Which the emerald waves at your feet gladly threw.

For, indeed, 'tis a sweet and peculiar pleasure,
(And blissful is he who such happiness finds,)
To possess but a span of the hour of leisure,
In elegant, pure, and aerial minds.

On receiving a curious Shell
From the same Ladies
(1817)

Hast thou from the caves of Golconda, a gem
Pure as the ice-drop that froze on the mountain?
Bright as the humming-bird's green diadem,
When it flutters in sun-beams that shine through a fountain?

Hast thou a goblet for dark sparkling wine?
That goblet right heavy, and massy, and gold?
And splendidly mark'd with the story divine
Of Armida the fair, and Rinaldo the bold?

Hast thou a steed with a mane richly flowing?
Hast thou a sword that thine enemy's smart is?
Hast thou a trumpet rich melodies blowing?
And wear'st thou the shield of the fam'd Britomartis?

What is it that hangs from thy shoulder, so brave,
Embroidered with many a spring peering flower?
Is it a scarf that thy fair lady gave?
And hastest thou now to that fair lady's bower?

Ah! courteous Sir Knight, with large joy thou art crown'd;
Full many the glories that brighten thy youth!
I will tell thee my blisses, which richly abound
In magical powers to bless, and to sooth.

On this scroll thou seest written in characters fair
A sun-beamy tale of a wreath, and a chain;
And, warrior, it nurtures the property rare
Of charming my mind from the trammels of pain.

This canopy mark: 'tis the work of a fay;
Beneath its rich shade did King Oberon languish,
When lovely Titania was far, far away,
And cruelly left him to sorrow, and anguish.

There, oft would he bring from his soft sighing lute
Wild strains to which, spell-bound, the nightingales listened;
The wondering spirits of heaven were mute,
And tears 'mong the dewdrops of morning oft glistened.

In this little dome, all those melodies strange,
Soft, plaintive, and melting, for ever will sigh;
Nor e'er will the notes from their tenderness change;
Nor e'er will the music of Oberon die.

So, when I am in a voluptuous vein,
I pillow my head on the sweets of the rose,
And list to the tale of the wreath, and the chain,
Till its echoes depart; then I sink to repose.

Adieu, valiant Eric! with joy thou art crown'd;
Full many the glories that brighten thy youth,
I too have my blisses, which richly abound
In magical powers, to bless and to sooth.

Epistle: To my Brother George
(1816)

Full many a dreary hour have I past,
My brain bewilder'd, and my mind o'ercast
With heaviness; in seasons when I've thought
No spherey strains by me could e'er be caught
From the blue dome, though I to dimness gaze
On the far depth where sheeted lightning plays;
Or, on the wavy grass outstretch'd supinely,
Pry 'mong the stars, to strive to think divinely:
That I should never hear Apollo's song,
Though feathery clouds were floating all along
The purple west, and, two bright streaks between,
The golden lyre itself were dimly seen:
That the still murmur of the honey bee
Would never teach a rural song to me:
That the bright glance from beauty's eyelids slanting
Would never make a lay of mine enchanting
Or warm my breast with ardour to unfold
Some tale of love and arms in time of old.

But there are times, when those that love the bay,
Fly from all sorrowing far, far away;
A sudden glow comes on them, nought they see
In water, earth, or air, but poesy.
It has been said, dear George, and true I hold it,
(For knightly Spenser to Libertas told it,)
That when a Poet is in such a trance,
In air he sees white coursers paw, and prance,
Bestridden of gay knights, in gay apparel,
Who at each other tilt in playful quarrel,
And what we, ignorantly, sheet-lightning call,
Is the swift opening of their wide portal,
When the bright warder blows his trumpet clear,
Whose tones reach nought on earth but Poet's ear.
When these enchanted portals open wide,
And through the light the horsemen swiftly glide,
The Poet's eye can reach those golden halls,
And view the glory of their festivals:
Their ladies fair, that in the distance seem
Fit for the silv'ring of a seraph's dream;
Their rich brimm'd goblets, that incessant run
Like the bright spots that move about the sun;
And, when upheld, the wine from each bright jar
Pours with the lustre of a falling star.
Yet further off, are dimly seen their bowers,

Of which, no mortal eye can reach the flowers;
And 'tis right just, for well Apollo knows
'Twould make the Poet quarrel with the rose.
All that's reveal'd from that far seat of blisses,
Is, the clear fountains' interchanging kisses,
As gracefully descending, light and thin,
Like silver streaks across a dolphin's fin,
When he upswimmeth from the coral caves,
And sports with half his tail above the waves.

These wonders strange he sees, and many more,
Whose head is pregnant with poetic lore.
Should he upon an evening ramble fare
With forehead to the soothing breezes bare,
Would he naught see but the dark, silent blue
With all its diamonds trembling through and through?
Or the coy moon, when in the waviness
Of whitest clouds she does her beauty dress,
And staidly paces higher up, and higher,
Like a sweet nun in holy-day attire?
Ah, yes! much more would start into his sight –
The revelries, and mysteries of night:
And should I ever see them, I will tell you
Such tales as needs must with amazement spell you.
These are the living pleasures of the bard:

But richer far posterity's award.
What does he murmur with his latest breath,
While his proud eye looks through the film of death?
What though I leave this dull, and earthly mould,
Yet shall my spirit lofty converse hold
With after times. – The patriot shall feel
My stern alarum, and unsheath his steel;
Or, in the senate thunder out my numbers
To startle princes from their easy slumbers.
The sage will mingle with each moral theme
My happy thoughts sententious; he will teem
With lofty periods when my verses fire him,
And then I'll stoop from heaven to inspire him.
Lays have I left of such a dear delight
That maids will sing them on their bridal night.
Gay villagers, upon a morn of May,
When they have tired their gentle limbs with play,
And form'd a snowy circle on the grass,
And plac'd in midst of all that lovely lass
Who chosen is their queen,– with her fine head
Crownèd with flowers purple, white, and red:
For there the lily, and the musk-rose, sighing,
Are emblems true of hapless lovers dying:
Between her breasts, that never yet felt trouble,
A bunch of violets full blown, and double,

Serenely sleep:– she from a casket takes
A little book,– and then a joy awakes
About each youthful heart,– with stifled cries,
And rubbing of white hands, and sparkling eyes:
For she's to read a tale of hopes, and fears;
One that I foster'd in my youthful years:
The pearls, that on each glist'ning circlet sleep,
Gush ever and anon with silent creep,
Lured by the innocent dimples. To sweet rest
Shall the dear babe, upon its mother's breast,
Be lull'd with songs of mine. Fair world, adieu!
Thy dales, and hills, are fading from my view:
Swiftly I mount, upon wide spreading pinions,
Far from the narrow bounds of thy dominions.
Full joy I feel, while thus I cleave the air,
That my soft verse will charm thy daughters fair,
And warm thy sons!– Ah, my dear friend and brother,
Could I, at once, my mad ambition smother,
For tasting joys like these, sure I should be
Happier, and dearer to society.
At times, 'tis true, I've felt relief from pain
When some bright thought has darted through my brain:
Through all that day I've felt a greater pleasure
Than if I'd brought to light a hidden treasure.
As to my sonnets, though none else should heed them,

I feel delighted, still, that you should read them.
Of late, too, I have had much calm enjoyment,
Stretch'd on the grass at my best lov'd employment
Of scribbling lines for you. These things I thought
While, in my face, the freshest breeze I caught.
E'en now I'm pillow'd on a bed of flowers
That crowns a lofty clift, which proudly towers
Above the ocean-waves. The stalks, and blades,
Chequer my tablet with their quivering shades.
On one side is a field of drooping oats,
Through which the poppies show their scarlet coats;
So pert and useless, that they bring to mind
The scarlet coats that pester human-kind.
And on the other side, outspread, is seen
Ocean's blue mantle streak'd with purple, and green.
Now 'tis I see a canvas'd ship, and now
Mark the bright silver curling round her prow.
I see the lark down-dropping to his nest,
And the broad winged sea-gull never at rest;
For when no more he spreads his feathers free,
His breast is dancing on the restless sea.
Now I direct my eyes into the west,
Which at this moment is in sunbeams drest:
Why westward turn? 'Twas but to say adieu!
'Twas but to kiss my hand, dear George, to you!

Sonnet: To my Brother George
(1817)

Many the wonders I this day have seen:
The sun, when first he kist away the tears
That fill'd the eyes of morn; – the laurel'd peers
Who from the feathery gold of evening lean;–
The ocean with its vastness, its blue green,
Its ships, its rocks, its caves, its hopes, its fears,–
Its voice mysterious, which whoso hears
Must think on what will be, and what has been.
E'en now, dear George, while this for you I write,
Cynthia is from her silken curtains peeping
So scantly, that it seems her bridal night,
And she her half-discover'd revels keeping.
But what, without the social thought of thee,
Would be the wonders of the sky and sea?

Sonnet: To My Brothers
(1816)

Small, busy flames play through the fresh laid coals,
And their faint cracklings o'er our silence creep
Like whispers of the household gods that keep
A gentle empire o'er fraternal souls.
And while, for rhymes, I search around the poles,
Your eyes are fix'd, as in poetic sleep,
Upon the lore so voluble and deep,
That aye at fall of night our care condoles.
This is your birth-day Tom, and I rejoice
That thus it passes smoothly, quietly.
Many such eves of gently whisp'ring noise
May we together pass, and calmly try
What are this world's true joys,– ere the great voice,
From its fair face, shall bid our spirits fly.

To a Friend who sent me some Roses
(1817)

As late I rambled in the happy fields,
What time the sky-lark shakes the tremulous dew
From his lush clover covert; – when anew
Adventurous knights take up their dinted shields:
I saw the sweetest flower wild nature yields,
A fresh-blown musk-rose; 'twas the first that threw
Its sweets upon the summer: graceful it grew
As is the wand that queen Titania wields.
And, as I feasted on its fragrancy,
I thought the garden-rose it far excell'd:
But when, O Wells! thy roses came to me
My sense with their deliciousness was spell'd:
Soft voices had they, that with tender plea
Whisper'd of peace, and truth, and friendliness unquell'd.

To one who has been long in city pent
(1817)

To one who has been long in city pent,
'Tis very sweet to look into the fair
And open face of heaven,– to breathe a prayer
Full in the smile of the blue firmament.
Who is more happy, when, with hearts content,
Fatigued he sinks into some pleasant lair
Of wavy grass, and reads a debonair
And gentle tale of love and languishment?
Returning home at evening, with an ear
Catching the notes of Philomel,– an eye
Watching the sailing cloudlet's bright career,
He mourns that day so soon has glided by:
E'en like the passage of an angel's tear
That falls through the clear ether silently.

Addressed to Haydon
(1817)

Highmindedness, a jealousy for good,
A loving-kindness for the great man's fame,
Dwells here and there with people of no name,
In noisome alley, and in pathless wood:
And where we think the truth least understood,
Oft may be found a 'singleness of aim',
That ought to frighten into hooded shame
A money mong'ling, pitiable brood.
How glorious this affection for the cause
Of stedfast genius, toiling gallantly!
What when a stout unbending champion awes
Envy, and Malice to their native sty?
Unnumber'd souls breathe out a still applause,
Proud to behold him in his country's eye.

Addressed to the Same
(1817)

Great spirits now on earth are sojourning;
He of the cloud, the cataract, the lake,
Who on Helvellyn's summit, wide awake,
Catches his freshness from Archangel's wing:
He of the rose, the violet, the spring,
The social smile, the chain for Freedom's sake:
And lo!- whose stedfastness would never take
A meaner sound than Raphael's whispering.
And other spirits there are standing apart
Upon the forehead of the age to come;
These, these will give the world another heart,
And other pulses. Hear ye not the hum
Of mighty workings? –

On the Grasshopper and Cricket
(1816)

The poetry of earth is never dead:
When all the birds are faint with the hot sun,
And hide in cooling trees, a voice will run
From hedge to hedge about the new-mown mead;
That is the Grasshopper's – he takes the lead
In summer luxury,– he has never done
With his delights; for when tired out with fun
He rests at ease beneath some pleasant weed.
The poetry of earth is ceasing never:
On a lone winter evening, when the frost
Has wrought a silence, from the stove there shrills
The Cricket's song, in warmth increasing ever,
And seems to one in drowsiness half lost,
The Grasshopper's among some grassy hills.

Written on the day that Mr Leigh Hunt left Prison
(1817)

What though, for showing truth to flatter'd state,
Kind Hunt was shut in prison, yet has he,
In his immortal spirit, been as free
As the sky-searching lark, and as elate.
Minion of grandeur! think you he did wait?
Think you he nought but prison walls did see,
Till, so unwilling, thou unturn'dst the key?
Ah, no! far happier, nobler was his fate!
In Spenser's halls he strayed, and bowers fair,
Culling enchanted flowers; and he flew
With daring Milton through the fields of air:
To regions of his own his genius true
Took happy flights. Who shall his fame impair
When thou art dead, and all thy wretched crew?

Happy is England! I could be content
(1817)

Happy is England! I could be content
To see no other verdure than its own;
To feel no other breezes than are blown
Through its tall woods with high romances blent:
Yet do I sometimes feel a languishment
For skies Italian, and an inward groan
To sit upon an Alp as on a throne,
And half forget what world or worldling meant.
Happy is England, sweet her artless daughters;
Enough their simple loveliness for me,
Enough their whitest arms in silence clinging:
Yet do I often warmly burn to see
Beauties of deeper glance, and hear their singing,
And float with them about the summer waters.

Robin Hood
To a Friend
(1820)

No! those days are gone away,
And their hours are old and grey,
And their minutes buried all
Under the down-trodden pall
Of the leaves of many years:
Many times have winter's shears,
Frozen North, and chilling East,
Sounded tempests to the feast
Of the forest's whispering fleeces,
Since men knew nor rent nor leases.

No, the bugle sounds no more,
And the twanging bow no more;
Silent is the ivory shrill
Past the heath and up the hill;
There is no mid-forest laugh,
Where lone Echo gives the half
To some wight, amaz'd to hear
Jesting, deep in forest drear.

On the fairest time of June
You may go, with sun or moon,
Or the seven stars to light you,
Or the polar ray to right you;
But you never may behold
Little John, or Robin bold;
Never one, of all the clan,
Thrumming on an empty can
Some old hunting ditty, while
He doth his green way beguile
To fair hostess Merriment,
Down beside the pasture Trent;
For he left the merry tale
Messenger for spicy ale.

Gone, the merry morris din;
Gone, the song of Gamelyn;
Gone, the tough-belted outlaw
Idling in the 'grenè shawe';
All are gone away and past!
And if Robin should be cast
Sudden from his turfèd grave,
And if Marian should have
Once again her forest days,
She would weep, and he would craze:

He would swear, for all his oaks,
Fall'n beneath the dockyard strokes,
Have rotted on the briny seas;
She would weep that her wild bees
Sang not to her – strange! that honey
Can't be got without hard money!

So it is: yet let us sing,
Honour to the old bow-string!
Honour to the bugle-horn!
Honour to the woods unshorn!
Honour to the Lincoln green!
Honour to the archer keen!
Honour to tight Little John,
And the horse he rode upon!
Honour to bold Robin Hood,
Sleeping in the underwood!
Honour to Maid Marian,
And to all the Sherwood-clan!
Though their days have hurried by,
Let us two a burden try.

Lines on the Mermaid Tavern
(1820)

Souls of Poets dead and gone,
What Elysium have ye known,
Happy field or mossy cavern,
Choicer than the Mermaid Tavern?
Have ye tippled drink more fine
Than mine host's Canary wine?
Or are fruits of Paradise
Sweeter than those dainty pies
Of venison? O generous food!
Drest as though bold Robin Hood
Would, with his maid Marian,
Sup and bowse from horn and can.

I have heard that on a day
Mine host's sign-board flew away,
Nobody knew whither, till
An astrologer's old quill
To a sheepskin gave the story,
Said he saw you in your glory,

Underneath a new old-sign
Sipping beverage divine,
And pledging with contented smack
The Mermaid in the Zodiac.

Souls of Poets dead and gone,
What Elysium have ye known,
Happy field or mossy cavern,
Choicer than the Mermaid Tavern?

Sonnet: On the Sea

It keeps eternal whisperings around
Desolate shores, and with its mighty swell
Gluts twice ten thousand Caverns, till the spell
Of Hecate leaves them their old shadowy sound.
Often 'tis in such gentle temper found,
That scarcely will the very smallest shell
Be mov'd for days from where it sometime fell,
When last the winds of Heaven were unbound.
Oh ye! who have your eye-balls vex'd and tir'd,
Feast them upon the wideness of the Sea;
Oh ye! who have your eye-balls vex'd and tir'd,
Feast them upon the wideness of the Sea;
Oh ye! whose ears are dinn'd with uproar rude,
Or fed too much with cloying melody –
Sit ye near some old Cavern's Mouth, and brood
Until ye start, as if the sea-nymphs quir'd!

The Poet
A Fragment

Where's the Poet? show him! show him,
Muses nine! that I may know him!
'Tis the man who with a man
Is an equal, be he King,
Or poorest of the beggar-clan,
Or any other wondrous thing
A man may be 'twixt ape and Plato;
'Tis the man who with a bird,
Wren or Eagle, finds his way to
All its instincts; he hath heard
The Lion's roaring, and can tell
What his horny throat expresseth,
And to him the Tiger's yell
Comes articulate and presseth
On his ear like mother-tongue.

A draught of Sunshine

Hence Burgundy, Claret, and Port,
Away with old Hock and Madeira,
Too earthly ye are for my sport;
There's a beverage brighter and clearer.
Instead of a pitiful rummer,
My wine overbrims a whole summer;
My bowl is the sky,
And I drink at my eye,
Till I feel in the brain
A Delphian pain –
Then follow, my Caius! then follow:
On the green of the hill
We will drink our fill
Of golden sunshine,
Till our brains intertwine
With the glory and grace of Apollo!
God of the Meridian,
And of the East and West,
To thee my soul is flown,
And my body is earthward press'd. –
It is an awful mission,
A terrible division;

And leaves a gulph austere
To be fill'd with worldly fear.
Aye, when the soul is fled
To high above our head,
Affrighted do we gaze
After its airy maze,
As doth a mother wild,
When her young infant child
Is in an eagle's claws –
And is not this the cause
Of madness? – God of Song,
Thou bearest me along
Through sights I scarce can bear:
O let me, let me share
With the hot lyre and thee,
The staid Philosophy.
Temper my lonely hours,
And let me see thy bowers
More unalarm'd!

Sonnet to the Nile

Son of the old moon-mountains African!
Chief of the Pyramid and Crocodile!
We call thee fruitful, and, that very while,
A desert fills our seeing's inward span;
Nurse of swart nations since the world began,
Art thou so fruitful? or dost thou beguile
Such men to honour thee, who, worn with toil,
Rest for a space 'twixt Cairo and Decan?
O may dark fancies err! they surely do;
'Tis ignorance that makes a barren waste
Of all beyond itself, thou dost bedew
Green rushes like our rivers, and dost taste
The pleasant sun-rise, green isles hast thou too,
And to the sea as happily dost haste.

Sonnet: Written in Disgust of Vulgar Superstition

The church bells toll a melancholy round,
Calling the people to some other prayers,
Some other gloominess, more dreadful cares,
More harkening to the sermon's horrid sound.
Surely the mind of man is closely bound
In some black spell; seeing that each one tears
Himself from fireside joys, and Lydian airs,
And converse high of those with glory crown'd
Still, still they too, and I should feel a damp, –
A chill as from a tomb, did I not know
That they are dying like an outburnt lamp;
That 'tis their sighing, wailing ere they go
Into oblivion; – that fresh flowers will grow,
And many glories of immortal stamp.

Fragment of an Ode to Maia, written on May Day, 1818

Mother of Hermes! and still youthful Maia!
May I sing to thee
As thou was hymned on the shores of Baiæ?
Or may I woo thee
In earlier Sicilan? or thy smiles
Seek as they once were sought, in Grecian isles,
By Bards who died content on pleasant sward,
Leaving great verse unto a little clan?
O give me their old vigour, and unheard,
Save of the quiet Primrose, and the span
Of Heaven and few ears
Rounded by thee My song should die away
Content as theirs
Rich in the simple worship of a day. –

A prophecy: To George Keats in America

'Tis 'the witching time of night'
Orbèd is the Moon and bright
And the Stars they glisten, glisten
Seeming with bright eyes to listen
For what listen they?
For a song and for a charm
See they glisten in alarm
And the Moon is waxing warm
To hear what I shall say.
Moon keep wide thy golden ears
Hearken Stars, and hearken Spheres
Hearken thou eternal Sky
I sing an infant's lullaby
A pretty Lullaby!
Listen, Listen, listen, listen
Glisten, glisten, glisten, glisten
And hear my lullaby!
Though the Rushes that will make
Its cradle still are in the lake:
Though the linen then that will be
Its swathe is on the cotton tree;
Though the woollen that will keep
It warm, is on the sille sheep;

Listen, Stars, light, listen, listen,
Glisten, glisten, glisten, glisten
And hear my lullaby!
Child! I see thee! Child I've found thee!
Midst of the quiet all around thee!
Child I see thee! Child I spy thee
And thy mother sweet is nigh thee! –
Child I know thee! Child no more
But a Poet *ever*more
See, See the Lyre, the Lyre
In a flame of fire
Upon the little cradle's top
Flaring, flaring, flaring
Past the eyesight's bearing –
Awake it from its sleep
And see if it can keep
Its eyes upon the blaze.
Amaze! Amaze!
It stares, it stares, it stares
It dares what no one dares
If lifts its little hand into the flame
Unharm'd, and on the strings
Paddles a little tune and sings
With dumb endeavour sweetly!
Bard art thou completely!

Little Child
O' the western wild
Bard art thou completely! –
Sweetly with dumb endeavour –
A Poet now or never!
Little Child
O' the western wild
A Poet now or never!

A Song of Opposites

'Under the flag
Of each his faction, they to battle bring
Their embryon atoms.' – Milton

Welcome joy, and welcome sorrow,
Lethe's weed and Hermes' feather;
Come to-day, and come to-morrow,
I do love you both together!
I love to mark sad faces in fair weather;
And hear a merry laugh amid the thunder;
Fair and foul I love together.
Meadows sweet where flames are under,
And a giggle at a wonder;
Visage sage at pantomine;
Funeral, and steeple-chime;
Infant playing with a skull;
Morning fair, and shipwreck'd hull;
Nightshade with the woodbine kissing;
Serpents in red roses hissing;
Cleopatra regal-dress'd
With the aspic at her breast;
Dancing music, music sad,
Both together, sane and mad;

Muses bright and muses pale;
Sombre Saturn, Momus hale; –
Laugh and sigh, and laugh again;
Oh the sweetness of the pain!
Muses bright, and muses pale,
Bare your faces of the veil;
Let me see; and let me write
Of the day, and of the night –
Both together: – let me slake
All my thirst for sweet heart-ache!
Let my bower be of yew,
Interwreath'd with myrtles new;
Pines and lime-trees full in bloom,
And my couch a low grass-tomb.

Sonnet to a lady seen for a few Moments at Vauxhall

Time's sea hath been five years at its slow ebb,
Long hours have to and fro let creep the sand,
Since I was tangled in thy beauty's web,
And snared by the ungloving of thine hand.
And yet I never look on midnight sky,
But I behold thine eyes' well memory'd light;
I cannot look upon the rose's dye,
But to thy cheek my soul doth take its flight.
I cannot look on any budding flower,
But my fond ear, in fancy at thy lips
And hearkening for a love-sound, doth devour
Its sweets in the wrong sense: – Thou dost eclipse
Every delight with sweet remembering,
And grief unto my darling joys dost bring.

Ode to Apollo

In thy western halls of gold
When thou sittest in thy state,
Bards, that erst sublimely told
Heroic deeds, and sang of fate,
With fervour seize their adamantine lyres,
Whose chords are solid rays, and twinkle radiant fires.

Here Homer with his nervous arms
Strikes the twanging harp of war,
And even the western splendour warms,
While the trumpets sound afar:
But, what creates the most intense surprise,
His soul looks out through renovated eyes.

Then, through thy Temple wide, melodious swells
The sweet majestic tone of Maro's lyre:
The soul delighted on each accent dwells, –
Enraptur'd dwells, – not daring to respire,
The while he tells of grief around a funeral pyre.

'Tis awful silence then again;
Expectant stand the spheres;
Breathless the laurell'd peers,
Nor move, till ends the lofty strain,
Nor move till Milton's tuneful thunders cease,
And leave once more the ravish'd heavens in peace.

Thou biddest Shakspeare wave his hand,
And quickly forward spring
The Passions – a terrific band –
And each vibrates the string
That with its tyrant temper best accords,
While from their Master's lips pour forth the inspiring words.

A silver trumpet Spenser blows,
And, as its martial notes to silence flee,
From a virgin chorus flows
A hymn in praise of spotless Chastity.
'Tis still! Wild warblings from the Æolian lyre
Enchantment softly breathe, and tremblingly expire.

Next thy Tasso's ardent numbers
Float along the pleased air,
Calling youth from idle slumbers,
Rousing them from Pleasure's lair: —
Then o'er the strings his fingers gently move,
And melt the soul to pity and to love.

But when *Thou* joinest with the Nine,
And all the powers of song combine,
We listen here on earth:
Thy dying tones that fill the air,
And charm the ear of evening fair,
From thee, great God of Bards, receive their heavenly birth.

Sonnet on sitting down to read *King Lear* once again

O Golden tongued Romance, with serene lute!
Fair plumed Syren, Queen of far-away!
Leave melodizing on this wintry day,
Shut up thine olden pages, and be mute:
Adieu! for, once again, the fierce dispute
Betwixt damnation and impassion'd clay
Must I burn through; once more humbly assay
The bitter-sweet of this Shakespearian fruit:
Chief Poet! and ye clouds of Albion,
Begetters of our deep eternal theme!
When through the old oak Forest I am gone,
Let me not wander in a barren dream,
But, when I am consumed in the fire,
Give me new Phoenix wings to fly at my desire.

Written on Top of the Ben Nevis

Read me a lesson, Muse, and speak it loud
Upon the top of Nevis, blind in mist!
I look into the chasms, and a shroud
Vapourous doth hide them – just so much I wist
Mankind do know of hell; I look o'erhead,
And there is sullen mist, – even so much
Mankind can tell of heaven; mist is spread
Before the earth, beneath me, – even such,
Even so vague is man's sight of himself!
Here are the craggy stones beneath my feet, –
Thus much I know that, a poor witless elf,
I tread on them, – that all my eye doth meet
Is mist and crag, not only on this height,
But in the world of thought and mental might!

Ode on Indolence

'They toil not, neither do they spin.'

I

One morn before me were three figures seen,
With bowed necks, and joined hands, side-faced;
And one behind the other stepp'd serene,
In placid sandals, and in white robes graced;
They pass'd, like figures on a marble urn,
When shifted round to see the other side;
They came again; as when the urn once more
Is shifted round, the first seen shades return;
And they were strange to me, as may betide
With vases, to one deep in Phidian lore.

II

How is it, Shadows! that I knew ye not?
How came ye muffled in so hush a mask?
Was it a silent deep-disguised plot
To steal away, and leave without a task
My idle days? Ripe was the drowsy hour;
The blissful cloud of summer-indolence
Benumb'd my eyes; my pulse grew less and less;
Pain had no sting, and pleasure's wreath no flower:

O, why did ye not melt, and leave my sense
Unhaunted quite of all but – nothingness?

III

A third time pass'd they by, and passing, turn'd
Each one the face a moment whiles to me;
Then faded, and to follow them I burn'd
And ach'd for wings because I knew the three;
The first was a fair Maid, and Love her name;
The second was Ambition, pale of Cheek,
And ever watchful with fatigued eye;
The last, whom I love more, the more of blame
Is heap'd upon her, maiden most unmeek, –
I knew to be my demon Poesy.

IV

They faded, and, forsooth! I wanted wings:
O folly! What is love! and where is it?
And for that poor Ambition! it springs
From a man's little heart's short fever-fit;
For Poesy! – no, – she has not a joy, –
At least for me, – so sweet as drowsy noons,
And evenings steep'd in honied indolence;
O, for an age so shelter'd from annoy,
That I may never know how change the moons,
Or hear the voice of busy common-sense!

V

And once more came they by; – alas! wherefore?
My sleep had been embroider'd with dim dreams;
My soul had been a lawn besprinkled o'er
With flowers, and stirring shades, and baffled beams:
The morn was clouded, but no shower fell,
Tho' in her lids hung the sweet tears of May;
The open casement press'd a new-leav'd vine,
Let in the budding warmth and throstle's lay;
O Shadows! 'twas a time to bid farewell!
Upon your skirts had fallen no tears of mine.

VI

So, ye three Ghosts, adieu! Ye cannot raise
My head cool-bedded in the flowery grass;
For I would not be dieted with praise,
A pet-lamb in a sentimental farce!
Fade softly from my eyes, and be once more
In masque-like figures on the dreamy urn;
Farewell! I yet have visions for the night,
And for the day faint visions there is store;
Vanish, ye Phantoms! from my idle spright,
Into the clouds, and never more return!

The Human Seasons

Four Seasons fill the measure of the year;
    There are four seasons in the mind of man:
He has his lusty Spring, when fancy clear
    Takes in all beauty with an easy span:
He has his Summer, when luxuriously
    Spring's honied cud of youthful thought he loves
To ruminate, and by such dreaming high
    Is nearest unto heaven: quiet coves
His soul has in its Autumn, when his wings
    He furleth close; contented so to look
On mists in idleness – to let fair things
    Pass by unheeded as a threshold brook.
He has his Winter too of pale misfeature,
Or else he would forgo his mortal nature.

Women, wine, and snuff

Give me women, wine and snuff
Until I cry out 'hold, enough!'
You may do so sans objection
Till the day of resurrection;
For bless my beard they aye shall be
My beloved Trinity.

Modern Love

And what is love? It is a doll dress'd up
For idleness to cosset, nurse, and dandle;
A thing of soft misnomers, so divine
That silly youth doth think to make itself
Divine by loving, and so goes on
Yawning and doting a whole summer long,
Till Miss's comb is made a pearl tiara,
And common Wellingtons turn Romeo boots;
Then Cleopatra lives at number seven,
And Antony resides in Brunswick Square.
Fools! if some passions high have warm'd the world,
If Queens and Soldiers have play'd deep for hearts,
It is no reason why such agonies
Should be more common than the growth of weeds.
Fools! make me whole again that weighty pearl
The Queen of Egypt melted, and I'll say
That ye may love in spite of beaver hats.

On Death

I

Can death be sleep, when life is but a dream,
And scenes of bliss pass as a phantom by?
The transient pleasures as a vision seem,
And yet we think the greatest pain's to die.

II

How strange it is that man on earth should roam,
And lead a life of woe, but not forsake
His rugged path; nor dare he view alone
His future doom which is but to awake.

INDEX OF FIRST LINES